SHAMELESS

BEAT and prose poetry

elliot m rubin

Library of Congress
Copyright November 2024
Paperback ISBN # 979-8-9990376-0-2
EPUB ISBN # 979-8-9922464-9-0

Library of Congress Control Number
2025910814

Published 2025

Published by
elliot m rubin
Monroe Twp. New Jersey

Dedication

To my grandchildren
Shane, Isabelle, Jonathan, Carter,
Alexandra, Melanie, Mollie, and Madison

In memory of my father

Herman S. Rubin
who wrote poetry, prayers and letters all his life

Preface

I believe poetry is to be read and understood by all, and it needs to be written, for the most part, in plain language for everyone's enjoyment.

Too often, poets write in-depth, penetrating poems where you need to be well-read and/or versed in literary minutia to appreciate the poetry, not this book or any of my writings. I try to write so everyone can enjoy a few moments of intellectual satisfaction without consulting a dictionary or encyclopedia all the time.

Disclaimer

This book of poetry is not intended to be read by prudes, political book-banning conservatives, and/or sexually inhibited and repressed small-minded dolts.

No human models were caught, used, or harmed in any way in making the cover; it is AI-generated, at random.

What is Progressive Beat Poetry

Progressive beat poetry is a type of poetry that goes against the usual rules and traditions. It discusses social, political, and cultural issues to make people more aware and push for change. Here are some key points about progressive poetry:

- **Questioning the Norms**: Progressive beat poets often challenge and question the main social, political, and cultural ideas of society. They dive into complex topics like race, gender, and power.
- **Voices and Inclusion**: This poetry style aims to give a voice to those who are often ignored. It highlights stories and experiences that don't usually get attention.
- **Thinking and Talking**: Progressive beat poetry makes readers think about more significant societal issues and encourages meaningful conversations. It aims to start discussions and inspire actions towards social justice.
- **Breaking the Mold**: Progressive poets often play with form and structure, moving away from traditional styles to express their messages better.

Progressive beat poetry seeks to break free from traditional poetic conventions and push the boundaries of language, space-as-art, and expression.

Charles Bukowski, Frank O'Hara, and, recently, the great contemporary Chilean poet Pablo Neruda have greatly influenced my writing.

Table of Contents

8

terri-ann

in her youth she was a free spirit
giddy and willing to take an adventure
nothing's out of bounds
she rode the wind and surfed her life
nobody ever could hold her down

until

that ride on his *fat-boy harley davidson*
down the *california* coast to *san diego*
wind blew in her hair, untamed,
they stopped in *sausalito* for lunch, and
a quick tattoo as a reminder of the day;
then sat by a cliff and overlooked the waves
breaking below

today, she felt something new, a longing
to be with him forever, except he was not
the stay-at-home type of guy she now desired —
nice enough, in a romantic spot, but he felt
nothing of the sort, left her there, alone

he hoped on his hog and drove off into the sunset
without her — then she hitched a ride
on an eighteen-wheeler heading to *san francisco*
where she once worked as a dancer and escort,
ready to start over again, although she's now
middle-aged, a little less agile, but still able
to strut her stuff into the VIP lounge for cash

juggling

when i was younger and foolish
i was able to juggle girls like balls
now i finally caught my last one
and didn't let you bounce away

love is a funny thing
i know women juggle men, too
some more than others
i don't think you're any different

never asked about your history
i really don't want to know
how many hearts you broke
or what your body count is

i'm not interested, nor do i care —
when you are in my loving arms
and your naked body embraces me
there are no other men in your life

we are like one, interlocked in lust
jealousy will never exist
the past is in the past, and
the present is our future together

janis joplin songs

raise your hand because
i need **a man to love**
maybe you can
get it while you can

i feel like a **flower in the sun**
all i want is **to love somebody**
i'm **a woman left lonely**
you broke a **piece of my heart**

try to get back together
me and bobby mcgee
trust me again
work me, lord

i need **one good man**
to go **down on me**
in a **mercedes benz**
during the **summertime**

move over in the back seat
don't be a **cry baby**
you have the **turtle blues**
i feel like a **ball and chain**

my coochi **has the kozmic blues**
when there's a **half moon** rising

religious experience

when we were teens
i found heaven
with my tattooed girlfriend —
when we kissed
tongues ritually danced
in a religious fervor

often
i was allowed to visit paradise
where my lips
fervently prayed for more

buddy, gas station dog

he lives in a small
third tier tiny town
near nowhere fast
surrounded by nothing
his home
a two-pump gas station
where cars come and go
yet no one ever hit him —
if tired
he settles down wherever,
doesn't matter if there is oil or grease
his shaggy, dark brown fur carries it well
until one day, six-year-old barry
decides to bring him home —
mom was in the shower
heard her son come in
ma, i brought a friend for dinner —
finished washing, she puts on a robe
walks out to see a huge, soiled, dirty dog
on her new ligh tan carpet —
saddened,
barry walks his pal
back to the garage
and his oil-stained bed

his walking stick

one day in august years ago
while on vacation in new england
there was a craft fair in a town square
a five-foot wooden staff was bought
it was a natural finish, with clear varnish,
and held him up on many a trek
in town
on a dirt path
nothing too strenuous
except when he met his lady friend
on the other side of the farmer's field
under the shade of a thickly leaved tree
when all three laid on a blanket
and only the wooden staff rested
    oh, the stories it could tell
    the secrets it heard
    the kisses it witnessed
    yet sworn to secrecy
    upon threats of kindling

mass

i rarely attend services
the damn wood benches are hard
think i caught hemorrhoids from church
the preacher is a tight-ass holy roller

today's service is different
my wife is in the front
in a beautiful cherrywood coffin
dressed in her favorite blue taffeta dress

usually, she sits next to me
helps me get up from kneeling
bum knees from college football
plus, arthritis doesn't help either

always sat near or next to me
we'd watch television at night
our freaking dog always between us
now i'm stuck with the mutt

my two daughters flew in for this
the older one hated her
i think she wanted to make sure,
can't blame her, always nagged her

she makes a few million naked online
the other one's a lawyer in hollywood
represents big shots in divorce lawsuits
including her own two failed ones

feels funny to be alone again
not sure what to watch anymore
she always held the channel changer
wonder how i'll cope

i do like a strong sweet pina colada

16

lovesick double-dutch

doctor, doctor
play with me
can't you see
my heart is spoken
don't let it be
affection needs more
then a mere love's token
doctor, doctor
operate now
my scars are red
my feelings dead
fix in me what my last lover said
hold me, hold me
ever so tight
release my love
with all your might
kiss me, kiss me
all over tonight
hold my body
oh, so tight
doctor, doctor
make me right
i need you to heal
to make me feel
take your tour
from head to heel
doctor, doctor
come to me quick
i'm tired of being
so damn lovesick

eggs

went to the market for a few things, kamala's
by the entrance giving out round *i told you so* buttons;
in the dairy aisle rows of eggs, dozens of damn eggs,
more expensive than anyone could eat or buy,
these eggs elected the stupidest president in history
who lied about lowering prices —
i wander in aisle five and saw vladimir,
he asks *where's my puppet boy   whose nose grows
from lies, deeply entangled in russian strings* —
i replied *he's in the stupid aisle,
shopping on the left side for dumb thoughts
and on the right side for rambling, too long,
dictator stream of consciousness speeches* —
i saw stalin by the siberian frozen food section,
he sent a lot of people there —
i'm sure the dumbest president ever is jealous
as he can only whisk citizens off streets, from school, to
send them to a south-american
tyrant's torture prison without *habeas corpus*
or any rights, while ignoring supreme court orders —
behind the market's service counter
fidel smokes a cuban cigar, gleeful
the imperialist-americans
are self-destructing their economy
with senseless, harmful tariffs —
outside the food market, a woman holds a
cardboard sign, scrawled in thick, black marker
                    will marry
                    buy me eggs

lost love

i see a dead tree in the woods
stripped naked, its greenery gone,
leaves lay silent on the ground
deaf to the songs of fowl
my heart cries, there was no funeral
it reminds me of our romance ending

blue skies, white puffy clouds,
your smile as bright as sun
i loved you with all the life i had
yet you chose to leave me
my love life ceased
like the dead, rotted red leaves
which lay in front of me
as i stand still, sorrily staring

years later, your memory is still vivid
the soft kisses to my cheeks
vibrate in my crying soul
there was no worm-eating compost
back then
only vibrant life blooming

with a majestic green forest
thriving all around it —
it now stands as in rigor mortis
lonely in death, as i am in life

steak

the butcher shop
is covered in sawdust
tiny bits of wood
sprinkled on the floor
to absorb excess blood
as the heavy cleaver bears down
chops into raw meat
cuts it into single slices
as the essence of a cow
slithers onto a butcher's block
to be stacked high, weighed,
wrapped in green paper and bagged

i wonder if the cow knew —
did it realize its death
would feed numerous families,
is this god's will —
can heaven open its gates
for a lowly cow
does an animal have a soul
does it feel pain and loss
is it destiny to die for us
as jesus did for our souls
so humanity can eat and live —
when i hug my granddaughter
i wonder if bovines feel love,
because we are animals too

francis

i knew him
probably as well as millions of others

i spoke to him often when i felt a need
knowing he never heard me

though many times it seemed like he did
as a lot of his views i agreed with

though we were of different faiths
i never discussed religion with him

because i felt i had no need
yet, he was like many men

who lost a love as a young man —
a career decision made by a woman,

not the one he loved, or
wanted to build a home with,

but her mother, who prevented
their relationship from blossoming

so he took the other path
he wrote his sweetheart about

and became a priest of the people

new orleans

at mardi gras, the
festival fun-floats float
down narrow, french colonial streets
between bare-breasted balconettes
who yell down for colored beads
to be thrown at them
while the happy public below
drinks, brings crowd chaos, and
police scamper to protect and prevent
while others dance, carouse, and
blues blasts boozy bar's doors
off their hinges

the parade of debauchery
slowly continues
while rings of colorful beads
decorate women's chests, both
covered and uncovered
by some shy, demur, chaste, and
reserved insulated girls
who are titillated by the wildness

first date

she wants to go swimming
asks me to take her to the beach
wants to be wet all over

told her *my beach is hot*
i'll need a really big cover
to protect my skin from danger

she likes to skirt peril
said *i don't need a blanket*
her body wants to feel my deep heat

as we near the water's edge
said she feels a little damp
right before strong waves hit us

the current rocks us back and forth
she fully experiences her desires
her body, and i   soak   in the wetness

we finish the beach experience
then dry off and part
i never saw her again, though i tried

missing you

i went to the sea again
to see if you're still there
at one long-ago summer's beach
where we first met and loved

i hoped, wished, desired, and
expected you to be there
but you weren't —
we were teenagers
first loves
no money,
met in private at night
under the boardwalk
on a blanket
while waves broke on the breakers
our love blossomed
your kisses orgasmic
embedded in my memory
one summer, seven decades ago

alas, past love is in the past
never rekindled
but occasionally still flickers
old men are such fools

old men are such fools

louisa

many might mention
she is a handsome woman
some say striking, too
but it doesn't matter to admirers
who pay to see her perform
at the follies in paris
with other showgirls
in various stages of undress every evening,
except monday,
when she does her household chores
in blue jeans, a high-buttoned blouse, and
two kids who tag along

without makeup, she's unrecognizable
to admirers who pay plenty
to watch her strut the stage
with bountiful bare breasts
prompting dreams and wishes
in men of a certain age
as she lives in a reality
of humdrum everyday life
while they function
in a bubble of unrealized desires

club house pizza

it's a pizza joint in the front
dining room in the rear
right by the entryway is a card table
with four older men playing cards
potbellied, bald spots combed over,
or a lousy toupee on top
this is their clubhouse
youngest guy, fifty
with his back to the door —
the owner facing who enters
his gun under the table
it's a survival technique
locals deliver pies all day
they're the new residents in the area
black and spanish young men and women
the few left-over, younger white guys
from the neighborhood who didn't move away
go out with empty pizza boxes
later come back
filled with cash
they collect debts for the owner;
if they have a problem
one of the older guys leaves the game
to collect the money the old-fashioned way
a broken bone or a few slaps to the face
they always pay what's owed
then, the brooklyn card game
can continue

pieces from places in california

entire communities
burned
destroyed
rubbled ruins everywhere
quickly
everyone ran away
everything abandoned
except pieces of memory
    deceased dad's sweatshirt
    grandma's scribbled recipes
    pearls mom bequeathed
not enough time to grab more
kids in the backseat with the dog
as yellow-red flames dance about
on both sides of the street
reach high into the sky
my colorful car paint singed black

need to start over in life
how i don't know
but we are alive, and
saved those pieces
close to our hearts

tomorrow?

the sun came up this morning
yet he only sees grey clouds
anxiety ridden
the world's problems bear down

why go on living today
yesterday is gone
tomorrow won't be better
the world is doom and gloom

his final sleep has its arms open
welcoming rest
as mental blinders
keep logic out of sight
while he treasures quiet, peace,
a gentle farewell
no gun or window-jumping
his relief is small
two bottles emptied with water
then a long nap
naked in bed
his trip back to compost
has begun

driving to north carolina

long drive to greensboro
on interstate 95
stopped for food
just past quantico
on a sunny day —
filled up with liquids
for myself and car
then left the rest stop
merged onto the highway
traffic stopped
accident ahead
all lanes blocked
bladder feels fine
no vehicle movement
bladder starts to feel full
traffic stalls
bladder pressure builds
squirm in seat
stuck in the middle lane
can't pull over
abdominal intense pain
P R E S S U R E   B U I L D S

uh oh

graveyards

trees cleared
dirt seeded
mounds flattened
a desolate place
where families eternally unite

elderly dead led a life
but many children didn't
their years counted on one hand
alongside young men and women
who served honorably
they all left a life unlived
with careers not yet realized

graveyards are not a place of life
only tears grow there to water the grass
their memories etched on stone
to friends and relatives they're known;
in years to come, names become just words
meaningless   when the dead are read

west 57th street

manhattan's an island nation unto itself
where whatever wanted
can be found
      somewhere
if you can't obtain it there
it's not made
even musical coffins are here
long and narrow, usually finished
in deep, dark, glossy black
with white and black keys
      formerly made of ivory
now plastic, the name
steinway emblazoned on the side

located in their piano showroom
you can walk between
handmade, exquisite instruments
each worth a fortune, every one
a different sound and keyboard feel
where you can try them out
      uninterrupted
to experience an experience
most people will never have

hip hop love

parties are fun
dangerous too
when relationships strain
under stress of booze

she has a dude home
yet dances cheek-to-cheek
while his hand roams her domes
till emotions start to rage

they wink and drink
till edge of probity
then rush to consummate
with lots of kisses   he ignores the mrs

who's home asleep, expects
him to tiptoe in without a peep
after her girlfriend gets dressed
and leaves early, then she can sleep

bus trip

on the front page of the folded tabloid under my arm
is a crooked politician who looks like the guy
standing next to me on the bus, except he's not guilty
of pimping his young female assistant to other
legislators to get their votes

the crease in the paper teases me with a headline
wife sleeps with
i'd have to unfold it to read the rest of the story
but the bus is packed, and the young woman standing in
front of me with huge breasts keeps rubbing into me as
the bus stops and goes; she looks up, smiles an inviting
smile, i think,
maybe she's the politician's assistant taking the bus,
i'm not sure, i smile and then ask her if she'd like to go
for dinner and drinks tonight; she places her hand on
my arm
thank you for asking, but i don't date grandpas
i smile, then leave at the next stop
frustrated
i didn't get off with her

washington dc

the dog got loose
it's a big, over-weight, orange dog

humps every female it can
while its family cheers him on

until it goes back inside
to a large, white dog-house

exhausted from doing it
and every morning, chases

small brown squirrels up trees
to rid his lawn of foreign invaders

fallen angel

he casts a black shadow
never gray
    depression follows
    rain clouds overhead
    people scatter
no one wants him near
his being sows fear
the angel of death
hunts too often
aim's always accurate
to the deathly ill
arrows cease pain
bring restful sleep
      forever

sunday services

silence
dead silence
nobody spoke
the religious service has a moment of quietude
two pews up, a young couple stood   then left —
we only began a few minutes ago; now they're gone
i think they expected something else
    instead of introspection —
although she is cute and worthy of inspection
she walks out   he follows five steps behind
i don't think he wants to leave,
but i'd follow her too
now it's been two minutes of quiet, and
i notice the red-headed widow one pew over —
it's been three years since he died, and
rumors have it she's dating a much younger man
some say so young he's her son's age —
i don't know about that
but she's a looker in her tight pink sweater —
i'm bored now; maybe i'll leave too
i've had enough of this not-talking stuff
think i'll grab a hot dog for lunch
then turn on a game
i think *real madrid* is playing *liverpool*
the bets are in, but i know one i'll win —
it's what that lucky guy gets tonight
from his cute girlfriend, that's why he follows her —
she has him on her leash, probably a black leather one,
lucky bastard

mythology – a love poem

in high school
she was my helen of troy
sequestered away
hidden from view
never allowed out of her protected walls
except school
where her beauty mesmerized everyone

she became my muse
an arms-length enamorization
dreams filled with her
heart filled with desire
reality unfilled
until she needed geometry help

i volunteered to tutor —
my trojan horse was
a math book

finally, i sat next to her
alone
in her home
where we were isolated
from other jealous admirers
inside her protective walls

having a shot with her

one ounce of amber fluid is eighty-proof
i don't imbibe often, as it's too much for me
my preference is something smoother
like her long black hair fanned on my chest
after an hour of fortitude and exhaustion
when the shot glass emptied, then refilled,
until the blackness of sleep begins; then ends
when dawn's alarm hastens us to dress
to leave behind our bliss, and rejoin
the workday trudge, waiting for evening
to refill a shot glass while our lips
cross the divide to mesh, then mush two
tongues tinged with whisky while an open
bottle stands witness as i raise my intentions
to her lovely luscious lips and sip in her
succor as much as i can while sober, then
i can relish my charcoaled double-barreled
kentucky bourbon whisky girl

poetic life

at birth, only a single letter

soon it grows to a word

it becomes a line when siblings come along

add another lovely line
and they become a couplet

but today polyamory
being popular
three, changes it to a tercet

when two couplets
become entwined
the couplets are now four
and form a merry stanza

together, ten words can start a sonnet line of dance

high school sweethearts

she was sixteen
a hot, real redhead
we dated for months
   in bed
then lost touch —
sixty years later
friends call me
told me the deal
   she died —
thought we had
a lifetime love that was real
but i couldn't share
her drive was too much
her curvy body wanted touch
of female love for a real rush
it overcame my heartfelt crush —
a phone call this morning
told me of dna
i didn't think there was a way
a young red-headed girl
from nowhere
blasts out of my past
to be here today
and intends to stay
in my heart
till i pass away

smile

she's divorced
bleach bottle-blond
waist-length long hair
bright white smile
shapely at forty
with a small belly
her online fan page
earns a million a year
where it shows nude videos
of her doing things
to her breasts, body
with various devices
some electrified
many would consider
obscene and extremely pornographic
yet viewers continue to pay
to watch her explicit movies
unaware
her adult twenty-something son
is the cameraman

rub a dub lovers

the lovers are in the tub
vigorously they'd rub
embraced tightly
closer than peas in a pod
endearing whispers
between dueling tongues
water splashes onto the floor
luckily, they'd locked the door
parents thought he was
                          outside
and their daughter
                          was alone

but her lover was definitely
                          inside

hunting moby dick

another day
another poem
poets write consistently
pursuing the elusive poetic white whale
hopefully found on my blank page
with groundbreaking words
awe-inspiring phrases
to be recited by others
hailed by critics
wishing endlessly
for stanzas to stand out
to be recognized
before a poet's final words
expire

summer nursery camp 1950

at four years old
a van picks me up
filled with other kids
to bring us to an urban camp
in brooklyn on a major street
it was a hot humid july day
with no air conditioning back then

they had a side yard
with swings, sea saws, and
at a fenced part in the rear
where sprinklers were located
my coed group
were undressed, totally naked
and went through the spritzers

boys' and girls' innocence exposed
we ran around outside nude
as older kids and adults gawked
some things are not forgotten
even seventy-four years later
back then
nobody complained
nobody arrested
nobody thought   years later
it would still be remembered
except in today's world
as adults, we'd screw till we collapsed
and still, nobody would care

poet missing

there once was a poet of note
whose rhymes did seem to float
from her lined handwritten book
my eyes could not help but look

her early life was quite askew
but she pulled herself together
and began her path anew
having broken a mental tether

travelled in all the nation's states
even foreign ones in summer
now married and with child
stopped writing, what a bummer

never

nonspeech can be hurtful
my parents never said it
though i knew they did
osmosis told me of love

maybe it's their upbringing
both first-generation-americans
their parents immigrated
to build a new life
learn a new language
to earn to support a family
words were not important
acts and deeds spoke loudly

felt it had to stop with me

my children hear it often
unabashedly
i tell them
i love you

existential

life is about living long
everyone has the same end
when or where is conjecture

our winter is only around the bend
enjoy a springtime walk as long as it is
regardless of sun, snow, or rain

life's weather has cycles
our stay here sometimes burns
it's not always easy or pleasant

enjoy the journey
as best you can
if and when the proverbial stuff
hits the fan

i never told you this

but you should know
in north atlantic seas
whales breach and blow
steady ships sail away
but sti tossed about
in riled waters
up and down
up and down
and if you go overboard
you will definitely drown
our love, the same
we belong together
on the same ship
named marriage

triad

holiday work party after five
all employees met at a bar
never saw this guy before
a new hire i was told
started to talk, nice enough
he's engaged to a surgical nurse
me too, i told him straight away

his girl is off saturday and sunday
that's when he sees her, every weekend
mine is off weekdays, therefore
i see her wednesday and friday nights

our girlfriends work at the same hospital
on the same surgical floor
and both requested a round diamond ring
both are also named wendi, with an i
let's call them, what a coincidence he said
    i'm sure they'll be surprised i replied with a smirk
he called her floor station
asked for two wendi's
head nurse told him
there is only one wendi

she is away on her honeymoon

on the bus

ride'n a greyhound to nashville
pass'n through small town country
two pump gas stations a plenty
attached to a dirty window grocery
a sleep'n big shaggy dog at the door
and local girls hang'n and smoke'n
wait'n for a boy to drive up fast
then hop in for a long night of fun

my music makes me cash to live on
often play'n small clubs and bars
with pickup backup bands
townsfolk two step'n when i sing
bar girls flirt and hang out later
pick of the litter as they see potential
i know their endgame isn't love or talent
but a lifestyle of jewels, cars, and live-ins
a gated backcountry mansion and barn

always check ID's for age, and with care,
i select a tonight date, although it's late,
yellow shade motel is every small town's paradise —
one town, one day, on my way to sing
i met a preacher's daughter who held back sin
swayed my soul to marry, she's a win, i
never looked back, went to grand ole opry,
my turn at the mike, they swooped and swooned,
applause loud enough to wake the dead
saw williams, cash, and kristoffeson smile'n
now i'm ride'n a tour bus, with a bed in the back

playtime

^{up}   down

^{up}   down

legs lift   ^{up}

legs stomp   down

arms   f l a i l   for balance
better girls keep them
at theirside
step   step
     step   step

double dutch ropes
swing over their heads

laundry

eleven at night everything slows down
as quarters drop into machines
they seem to sluggishly slide to start the wash —
after six the elderly matron leaves for home
and i fold clothes by myself, as upbeat music
plays from ceiling speakers to an almost empty store

mildred is here too, doing her married daughter's stuff
she can barely walk, bad knees, no insurance —
i told her to apply for help with our state
because she came from one without federal aid,
pain flashes from her face with each step
i watch her walk until the swirling colors behind glass
catch my eye tumbling and tumbling over and over

the back lights flicker, fluorescent bulbs wink, as
black rings at each end forecast their coming failure —
the rows of white washers parallel to dryers
cracked and stained folding tables set between —
midnight, drugged girls walk in to rest and warm-up
while their pimps sit in a warm leather mercedes,
the girls inside sit on a wooden bench, chain-smoking

ask me for quarters before they leave
to buy cigarettes at the machine, in exchange
for their special services, which i decline,
but i give them half of what they need
hoping someday they'll get clean and repay me
but i know, once they walk out, i'm not even a memory

august snow

edwina is a proud direct descendant
of early pilgrims from new england
who had strict puritan values —
she lives in brooklyn, near coney island,
in a respectable two-family home
the city's air is heavy, hard to breathe
in hot, humid august
with midcentury, stifling air pollution —
all snow and ice gone, except
for drug dealers called *snowmen*, and
she is the *snow-queen* of new york —
her office is on a surf avenue corner
a block from hotdog heaven —
young runaway girls collect cash,
others bring bags of drugs to their buyers —
as she safely oversees everything from
across the street, in case police pop up,
like they did two years ago, her girls
took the rap, jumped bail, fleeing
to puerto rico with edwina's help
because if they ratted on her, they knew,
once out, their lives were over

on sunday mornings
edwina always attends church

catch

a loving couple
married for decades
sit across from each other
as early morning news
drones on

she cuts open an apple
swipes peanut butter on a sliver
turns to him
with no emotion on her face
says
catch the knife

after he leaves the hospital
their lawyer visits her in custody
a court orders therapy —
bipolar is not an easy cure
and love is hard to walk away from

time

how do you capture
precious moments
    to replay them in your heart
    when the world stops
    and air smells of roses
the future
in front of you
holds you in its arms
when outside
    everything is chaos
    people die needlessly in wars
    life-saving vaccines vilified
and all you want
is to be loved

forever

time once spent is gone
tough to be repeated
the essence of love is timeless
once it burrows into your soul

heartache

i wish
i could peer through a window
to see what is in her heart
before we start a romance —
walking on manhattan's fifth avenue
high-end merchant's glass storefronts
display what is inside
this gives a hint of what to expect;
personal feelings she chose to hide
not openly displayed
everything is hidden,
no insight behind her smiles,
white teeth, and gentle words,
every normal person seeks love
and on tenth avenue in manhattan,
midtown love can be purchased
without expensive dinners,
broadway shows, and
a feathery thank you hug
never to see her again

her cat died

the orange tabby cat

caught a big black rat

after the rodent ate some bait

the feline sat and ate

as the meal did satiate

now there's a dead fat cat

and no big fat rat

senior dating

i'm seventy-nine. she is eighty, buried three husbands,
her body slightly rounded, big pendulous breasts
that flop down alongside her ribs when she wraps her
legs around my waist; suddenly, i'm in a western
cowboy rodeo as my mare bucks violently, tries to
throw me

i hold on best i can, knowing if i slide off my saddle, i'd
not be able to mount up again; then her left leg hit the
bed and turned us over; my bronco now rides me,
bucking violently, tiring me out till she falls back,
exhausted; her event finished, we both end panting,
trying to catch a breath

i lie still on her floral sheets till my wild filly leaves to
shower, drags me along to wash our sweat away when
the rain shower head explodes with a torrent, somehow
stimulates, and we exchange endearments once more —
at that moment, drained and fatigued, i now know why
her three husbands died, as being with her
i saw heaven

wayward husband

few remember him fondly
very little, nice things said
voiced praise at his passing
a saint if you heard their words

often most say out loud
they come to bury caesar, and
ensure he is dead and gone
not praise him   to high heaven

lord knows that's not where he's going:
an ugly drunk, gambler, adulterer,
he cheated in everything he ever did —
silently, they lowered the casket and smiled

he was shot in his married lover's bed
by two people   his enraged wife
who smiled with every shot, and his
lover's husband, who carefully aimed

they waited
  to call for help
    until he
        bled
            dead
with no breath left to shout out

hidden people

plucked off streets
by a syrian dictator
flung into a windowless
humid, stale air,
stifling to breathe
unsanitary prison
at eighteen,
innocent
family fraught with fear
year after year
asked everywhere
searched secret sources
yes, they have him
no, they don't
finally found
after the rebels freed thousands —
at fifty-eight, he walks out
bearded, blinded by sunlight
an older brother recognizes him
forty years gone
never lived a whole life
no wife,
no children,
no nothing
survival was his goal
while the jailer secretly flew away
for sanctuary in freezing russia
leaving relatives to rebel's mercy

city living

can you live in a city
while remaining a country kid

can black asphalt replace
the dark coal mines of youth
when rail cars moved north
and pieces fell off to heat our home

can bluegrass sung by granny
and uncle jedediah, on his violin
be replaced by urban tunes and soul
while i look up and can't see any clouds

as city smog and pollution hide the sun
which warms cold forest creeks
where we bare-ass swam on hot july days
then dry off on a blanket tightly enwrapped

gently rolling treed hills are a memory
replaced by skyscrapers of steel and glass
i won't die here   health care's better than
back home, where the doctor came twice a year

but given a choice of where to rest forever
bury me in the green glen back home
birds can sing to me, children run barefoot
over my final bed   tranquilly is desired

i miss it

20% more died

humid, tepid, summer air
closed-up building entrance
windows shattered
electric turned off
lead paint peels off walls
abandoned by owner
yet inhabited
by derelicts,
addicts, homeless,
and immigrants

police report
more people died
in this location
than last year;
yet nothing is done

they're throwaway bodies
yet alive
in the fog of life

voices

i hear a voice in my mind
words
    spring to life
    they try to get out
my creativity struggles
to live outside my brain
and leave behind smiles,
appreciation, and
share satisfaction
on paper
while my pen writes
quickly
as the floodgates swing open
thoughts regurgitate
a lifetime of experience
shared poetically

reunion

when poets get together
they talk in metaphors
say one thing
mean something else

their speech is sweet
juicy as a georgia peach
they whisper at the meet
take their time to rhyme

ten syllables to a sentence
words fall into a sequence
nobody speaks on impulse
no words will repulse

meeting time does not fly
they drone on until they die

immigration and customs enforcement - ice

the door closes
a nation of immigrants
is no more
only white skin can enter
if they have the right religion
and the dictator-president-king
wakes up and doesn't know
where you came from
since he is undereducated

those caught
by racist stormtroopers
are jailed, flown to cuba
in chains, handcuffed, then
jailed with islamic terrorists

miss liberty in the harbor
lowers her bright torch
extinguishes it in the bay, as
huddled masses yearning to breath free
are repulsed, returned
to their misery
barred
from the land of opportunity
by white, pseudo christian nationalists

loveless valentine

olive skin
   white hair
     red eyes
       black nails
tender
   hands and kisses
her body has the requisite parts
   muscle memory makes
experienced love without effort
   in some things she surpasses youth
as her mature female form
   attracts suitors of all ages
but refrains from backseats
   and requires a five-star bedroom

in old age

we sit in front of the flames
in our rustic summer hideaway,
been together
fifty-five years

through glories and depressions
our fires still burn bright
yet i always wonder
who was in her hearth first

i never forgot mine

mountain climbing in manhattan

after thoroughly exploring
the damp cavernous cavern
located deep in a valley
he picks his head up
to peer through a thick thicket
and spots twin peaks ahead
their tops beckon action
hand over hand, his body crawls up
attempts to mount the two everests —
breathing heavily, labored, the
mountain tops within his grasp
his efforts are almost completed
but a misstep
    knocks him off
        quickly he glides
                down,
                    exhausted,
                        falls off

onto his back
onto her bed

that night

i remember it well
    our first meet
we danced till dawn
    venus whispered your name
cherubs floated around us
    i held an angel in my arms
our first kiss was sugar-sweet
    yearned for more
now our dance is done
    a lifetime of love almost over
i sit holding your hand in mine
    one last time
    one last kiss
will last forever

insurrection 2

prosecutors fired
agency watchdogs fired
tens of thousands fired
sycophants hired
unqualified placed in charge
power focused on the leader
armed force's generals decimated
national enemies given sway

finally, a beloved general
orders his special ops forces
to kill the fascist leader, the next in line,
and beholden agency heads, too

then orders national general elections

is the republic saved?

a fall ritual

every year as winter approaches
green leaves turn crimson with death
a strong wind forces release, and
they all decide to meet at my door

every morning, my wife sweeps the floor,
but the rascals keep coming back
the next day with even more!
her arms are tired, and her muscles sore

my home must be special
they love my front door
she piles them up on my yellowed lawn
but alas, they're back the very next dawn

diversity equality inclusion

close the drapes
the government is looking
they want everyone to be uniform

close the drapes
can't say you're different
doesn't matter if you are

close the drapes
ability counts, as it always has, and
those lesser in society can't achieve

close the drapes
generations of discrimination
continues to hold back talent

close the drapes
they deny opportunities, unless
you're white, and the right christian

close the drapes
they're out to get rid of woke
and me, we, and us

close the drapes
close the coffin
my country has died

juanita perez

she was brilliant
had brown skin
trekked up from mexico
couldn't get in

maga's think they're fighting sin
kept her out with razor-thin wire
threw her potential in the bin
her situation is now extremely dire

uncurables could've been cured
smart thinking kind of blurred
medical school was in her future
but congress acts as if in a stupor

smugglers buried her in desert sand
never took her to the promised land

goodbye

my poetry might soon end
i'm not twenty-one anymore
skipping, running, playing sports
are now fond memories of my youth

heart doctor told me my ticker's broke
like a car i'll soon need a valve job repair
the operation is now considered standard
but i'll still be subject to random screwups

aorta stenosis is the medical term
a stretched-out valve soon has to be replaced
forget the symptoms, they don't really matter
i still need to wake up without any blood clots

sixty years of marriage

it was a bright, sunny day
for a very dark event
a husband is buried
a widow grieves
not enough tissues to
mop up tears
friends and family fly in
funeral home overflows

for decades deceased
was an activist in his community
too many accolades to list
two mayors come to bury one
four police cars with lights flashing
led the hearse for miles
while god anxiously waits
at the cemetery gates
for the procession

In the past and present

in the past,
things were great —
girls skipping rope
white picket fence as in primers
dick, jane, and spot frolic in streets
nothing bad ever happened to us

today,
the world falls apart —
everyday something else happens
people die, women are raped and killed
wars more deadly and more often
seems everything happens to us

truth be told,
nothing has changed —
life's still filled with things we detest
except news travels faster
modern tech brings visuals into homes,
in living color, too

hair-wash girls

decades ago,
when i had a full head of hair,
there was an upscale barber shop
i would frequent when needed

they had young women
who were blessed with big breasts
in sheer body-hugging tee shirts
bent over to wash your hair

a small protrusion teased men's lips
only millimeters from touching
unless you were young and good-looking
obviously, there were large tips

letters of love

there's no wind
softly snowflakes settle
outside, everything's blanketed
inside, i sip coffee
while my date next to me
is in bed asleep

next week
her dates's divorce will be final
my daughter is away
her mother has her today
just as well, her teacher,
after school's out   is here with me

she taught me the abc's of love
Always be there for them
Because love is a delicate snowflake
Care for them as you would yourself
Don't take someone for granted

that kid is ugly

sorry
i know i shouldn't say that

he's not thin or fat
small or tall

that kid is just really, really ugly
i know it's not politically correct to say

how can someone go through life that way
yet   he married the town's beauty queen

he might even be considered fugly
some would say he's very lucky

his personality's great
clothes are up to date

still, that kid is ugly
sorry

red carnival glass

the cupboard has an uneven number
of red kitchen glasses from my wife's grandmother
soldiered row after row, tightly packed, upright,
i take one to fill with black cherry soda

it feels cold when i drink from it
what table stories it can tell if it could speak —
the red lips that drank from it spoke in tongues
foreign to my ears when i heard them years ago

family and friends visited and used them
their ghosts relish the memories from those times
the lives lived and lost left imprints on me
to spring back to life when i pick up a glass

eighty years after its purchase, it now sits
on my red granite kitchen counter   alone
never joined with its siblings in the closet
only one glass used by me, never my wife

too many memories can't bring back the lost
their glasses sit put away in my home, rarely used,
except when red plastic cups are all gone —
soon the kids'll throw them away, muted, after we pass

donald gump

stupid is as stupid does forest gump

i'll lower egg prices on day one
the orange-tinted man
said not in fun
but the yoke is on him
with egg on his face
as his cheshire cat smile
and pinocchio nose
exposed his untold truths
his crossed fingers
and lies from his spittle lips
while prices spiral upward
along with revisited inflation
while billionaires save money
with unfair tax breaks
just for them
not for **US**a

he has riveting blue eyes

pressed her against the bed
both arms raised over her head
pulled aside long black hair
exposing her soft, supple neck
gently nibbles on an ear lobe
a hickey here, a hickey there
his lips glide over a slender body
until he finds paradise
as they move in unison
tightly entangled in unabated lust
they finally finish fetish love

she wants to write in her diary
about this latest exploit
as she usually does,
to eventually become a book
of her youthful exploits in new york city
but first, he places her in a wheelchair
before he leaves
as she wheels herself to a computer
where she figuratively
adds a notch to her belt

i don't want to be old anymore

running and skipping are now memories
waking up to walk to school *fades away*
breakfast is forgotten by noon
i remember things from the past
but not yesterday
my friends from youth have died
their names and faces clouded

in years to come i'll be a drizzle
instead of a hurricane in people's thoughts
eventually cease to exist
except as a nameless person
in pictures, strangers peer through
in an antique shop in a rural vermont barn
as a curiosity   and i'll become a question

song with her name played

our song came on the radio
as i was driving with my wife
but if wasn't *our* song
and she reminded me of that fact —
sixty-seven years ago, i dated this girl
when she was sixteen, i was seventeen —
it was a summer of love
she tried out for a beauty contest
ended up in the grand finals
of the miss teenage america contest
with her picture in a teen magazine —
at the end of august she went home to new jersey
i to brooklyn, only to see her christmas week —
she was friends with my sister, stayed at my home,
but that week was the last time we were together —
it was a fun week; we took up where we left off,
but it was not a forever thing, as she cheated
on her boyfriend with me during the summer, and
on that week of heaven in winter too —
i was her teen fling
it was over when she left,
what a way to go

the author at seventeen

pizza pizza

sits on a side street
in manhattan's
greenwich village
best pizza place in town
small tables
small chairs
store space is narrow width
and short length
long lines to get in
checkerboard tablecloths
deep fried dough
sauce and cheese imported
michelin rated
news stations feature it
reporters sit and savor slices
write raves over the taste
food fit for kings
local queens too
broadway stars visit
elbow in to sit
reservations not taken
outside lines grow longer
while pizzas bake'n
worth the wait'n

make **a**merica **g**roan **ag**ain - maga

don't endorse vaccines
not enough deaths from the pandemic
now, they might bring back
measles, covid, and even polio again

close the education department
don't set national standards
they want undereducated voters
keep kids dumb and stupid

cut back medical programs
too many poor people use it
let them get sick and die
saves a lot of cash for the rich

who needs social security
it's socialism and handouts
old people should live with family
reduces the deficit, saves money

eliminate income taxes for everyone
billionaires can save millions
add value-added sales tax
poor people proportionately pay more

maga – **m**aga america **g**roan **ag**ain

escape

five-year-old madison
a hurricane in pajamas
w. h i z z e s
through breakfast cereal
as a waterfall of milk
cascades down
a mountain of multicolored
sugar-squares to splash puddles
on a pink plastic tablecloth
similar to the backyard's lakes
where she cakes her clothes
on mother nature's muddy ground
chases butterflies,
and jumps
shouts *wait*
to fill the air with giggles and laughter
as the former caterpillar
struggles
to lift itself to safety   and
evade a death sentence
in a sealed glass bottle
brought into kindergarten
for a science day of show and tell

good girls

tend to be demure
dress conservatively
showing little exposed skin
their language proper
never a profanity or slur
kindness showered on everyone —
sexually naïve
they wait till marriage
no smoking or
drugs to get high
they are to be cherished
also, they never tell an untruth —
but to be honest with you
i really, really, really
prefer bad girls

teenage testosterone

didn't have his license or even any money
decided he'd settle for a fast girlfriend
but where could he find *that kind of girl*
a few blocks away was a gentleman's club —
inside, he knew were *those girls* he desired,
as he stood outside, he looked at pictures
hung outside of dancers who worked there —
he was underage and couldn't be admitted
and watched as wealthy men sauntered in —
he felt like he was standing in a rose garden
admiring the flowers, even their scent,
and knew he might be able to pluck one, yet
bouncers are there, they're the bushes thorns,
preventing his dream from fruition

fascism 2025

US immigration agents arrest Palestinian student protester at Columbia University in Trump crackdown – Reuters March 10, 2025

knock, knock
> *who's there*

immigration and customs enforcement (ICE)
> *why are you here*

the president said your husband is a terrorist
> *but he only led a peaceful protest at college*

tell him to come out now, or we're going in
> *he's coming; put your guns away*

place your hands behind your head .
> *where are you taking him*

guantanamo bay in cuba
> *do you have a court warrant*

don't need it, have a presidential warrant
> *this is not nazi germany, you know*

this is the new **u**nconstitutional **s**tates of **a**merica
and you better watch what you say

regrets

i'll never know
if i'm worthy enough now
for you to love me again
since we split years ago
i was young and immature
didn't appreciate your love

all i needed then
was booze and bitches
then i didn't have true love in me
cause i couldn't recognize it
through a drunken haze
but i'm sober now
all grown up and stuff

oh, how i long for you
to hold your hand again
and press it to my heart
but you were decades ago
and i lost you way back then
if only heaven could intercede
and bring you back to me

if only

brooklyn boxer

i don't remember his name
met him in a brooklyn store
he was tall, muscular, imposing man
with a short buzz haircut,
a gruff manor, no charming personality
and facial scars on a chiseled face

we had a short conversation
told me he is a retired boxer
now trains young men in the gym
and at night, works as a bouncer
in a dance club

his last professional fight
was one of george foreman's early ones
said hitting him was like
punching a tree trunk, and
in the first round
he knew he would lose

he retired after that bout
i can't imagine anyone
getting into a ring with this guy
and he not winning
yet the champ
knocked him out

too soon

what's the right amount of time
before you move on, it's no crime —
how long do you wait
before going on a first date

maybe your life's love died
too many tear tissues dried
sadness and grief are tough
time moves on; yes, it's rough

when dating someone you like
then discover she's a bi-dyke —
if monogamy is your thing
you find out you're only a fling

remember, it's never too soon
your heart deserves a full moon
move on, and don't look back
don't give life lived any slack

remember, this is your only journey
travel it with gusto, not on a gurney

lines and wrinkles

it is only clean skin
a foundation born smooth
no facial crevices
or teen pimples

as age creeps upward
elements attack
pores clog, scars appear
eyelids start to droop
chin skin fills and sags
lines appear   where none existed

the beauty of youth gone
facial features flounder
elderly faces filled with lines,
liver spots, moles, and eczema
then hair thins, face skin
extends to the top of your head

your mirror sheds your youth
it's long gone, never to reappear
as we age
only true love continues
it never leaves us

i will always be with you

a dying daughter

they don't teach this in school
how to cope with a self-destructing child
dad does what he thinks is best
but when a child takes drugs
    drugs take your child
his daughter's new name
is heroin, cocaine, or
whatever her pusher's pushing today

his hands are free   yet tied
the will to help stifled by law
the drugged daughter is dying
and there's not much to be done
she is:
an adult
a drug addict
a lost soul
a loving daughter
yet lost from life
and dying from drugs

at a middling motel

the white sheets aren't egyptian
and the carpet shows wear
happily, the mattress is not too soft
her fleshy arm draped across my bare chest
and her head snuggly nuzzled
in the crook of my neck
while her tongue licks it
as long-manicured fingernails   slowly
draw circles across my naked body

presidents' day's a school holiday
she's off work and spending it with me
while her husband is home
babysitting three raucous children
while she's supposed to be shopping
and enjoying some alone time

we are old friends who get together
every year for old time's sake —
to catch up and enjoy each other,
like bill clinton, we didn't have sex today
because she's trying for number four
and our time together is wild and raw
she wants to know who the father is;
so we kiss, cuddle, and….

when we leave, i drive her to a jewelry store
and buy her something, proof she had shopped

maggie

it is a sunny monday morning
her doctor arrives about noon
along with friends and family
they circle her bed

wears her late husband's shirt
with his favorite team logo
the physician asks
in front of witnesses

is today the day you wish to die

a fatal diagnosis given months before
now bedridden and firm in belief
she doesn't want to live vegetatively
and jokes with those who love her

five minutes after she drinks the brew
the thousand-dollar medicine
begins to put her to sleep
about an hour or so later, she

dies in peace in her bed
quietly, slowly, with dignity
no debilitating, drawn-out death
but at a time and place, she chose

grandma died at 92

weeks after the funeral
her son and daughter arrived
with grandchildren to empty the home
of furniture and everything else

her clothes were gathered to donate
papers and books dumped in bags
glassware and kitchen stuff sent to trash
when a favorite granddaughter stopped it

she had stayed with granny very often
knew she only ate on one small plate
it was round, blue, glazed ceramic with a design —
her mom and uncle didn't understand why

until the son took it to inspect
turned it over, saw his name and a year
scribbled on the underside;
he made it in school when he was seven

now seventy-four, he realized his mother
cherished it, and he gave it to his niece
who had helped her grandmother
in her last years, as a keepsake of love

clumps

when a bunch of whatever gets together
it can be called a lot of things: a
group, gathering, mob, congregation
but when cancer cells appear
i call it a clump
tumors in the human body
eat off living tissue   it can be deadly

sitting alone in the doctor's office
the iv-bag's elevated long thin tubing
running downward
the poison drips
         drips
         drips
         down
toward the inserted needle —
slowly
         time
                drags on
as the body absorbs it
        absorbs a demon killer
and the race is on
the cancer or body
which dies first

is determined in time

ambiguity solved

the dark clouds parted, and
at dawn, she finally awoke
and with a sledgehammer,
smashes down a closet door
and now openly faces the fear
she had dreaded for so long;
parents and friends never knew,
though some suspected —
now, being an adult
she doesn't just walk through
the opening with strong legs,
she dashes out into the world
exposes herself as loud,
proud and openly gay
who loves who she loves
and no longer hides herself
in the her mind's closet —
her husband knew
but kept it between them
as they had quietly been active
in secret swinger's groups for years
allowing her to taste bisexuality fully
until the basket of desire overflows
at those play sessions

fish out of water

trying to breathe with a hook in its mouth
it flips flops, over and over again
strains to fill its lungs until it lies still
motionless, dead, eyes wide, until removed

my grandmother, flat on her back in bed
motions me to come close, *give me a kiss*
she softly tells me in a hushed whisper
i kiss her cheek and then start to stand up

with great strain on her dying heart, she pulls
my face back down to hers, and kisses me
directly on my lips, then goes to sleep—
my mom moves me out of the cold bedroom

grandmother's marriage was of convenience —
there was no love, it was not an arranged
one either, but she did it to bring her
three younger siblings to america

she had promised her dying mother, on
her death bed, she'd take care of them all —
her fiancé lied about bringing them
over so she dumped him — on the rebound

his friend said he'd pay to help her bring them,
so she married him, and he kept his word —
grandma had two sons, a daughter (my mom)
and i was her daughter's first child, a son

there's a special relationship between
a mother and daughter, and firstborn (me) —
granny took me to school, fed me lunch daily
and i slept over often   in this bed

limerence

it was a really good love
true love, many would say
he was to be her husband, she
knew everything about him

as teenagers, they embraced;
often spent nights together
yet at school the next day
they would barely speak

when they split for college,
never returned home
and were not intimate ever again
but her desires never ceased

she dreamt of him each day
married twenty years to another, three kids,
and a loving husband in every way;
happily married, yet desired her old love

insatiable desires became a reality
her mind never could be rid of him
therapy helped cloud it a bit, but
her loins desperately continue to rumble

littering 1963

i used to smoke a parliament-brand cigarette,
filtered, and a little longer than some —
when finished, i'd stomp it out
twisting my shoe until it was smashed
then winds blew away charred remains
with the box in my pants pocket until it, too,
was empty —
then i'd toss it in the gutter and walk away
without thinking twice

susan from manhattan
was my summer fling that year,
we were seventeen,
dated and spent weeks together
until that day   when she went for a car ride
with a much older guy
in a chevrolet 409 convertible; she
discarded me, and my love littered all over
the street, crushed and vaporized into tiny nothings
and blown away
never to be put back
in the same way with her
ever again

i was her smoked cigarette

america 2025

our youth were sent to southeast asia
to fight for what was never made clear
their deaths and damage were very, very dear
forty years later, we still ask why they died

old men sent their young for honor and valor
left dead fifty-eight thousand dreams to rot,
for those they found, to ship back home, they're
buried in arlington's sacred ground

fighting wars, trade wars, people still won't win
narcissistic dictators believe they can't sin
they're always right, and the rest are wrong
women and children are the first to feel the pain

just leave things alone; don't mess with success
full employment, inflation down, look what he did
breaks laws, ignores courts, whisks men off the street
our democracy is dead, and elected traitors still sit

in a do-nothing congress filled with ignoble stooges
they ignore people's pain as they collect huge checks
and get full medical insurance while we say *hey,*
we sent you there to support and help us, **NOT HIM!**

richest man in the world

the fundamental weakness of western civilization
is empathy – elon musk

how did i miss these things

    musk college endowments
        for humanities
    musk pediatric and maternity
        wings at local hospitals
    musk school scholarships
        for underprivileged students
    musk nationwide food banks and
        home food deliveries for the elderly
    musk free nursing homes for indigent elderly
        with free daycare in poor neighborhoods
    musk vocational schools for the trades
        and free education for medical students

with so many projects,
i can't believe i *musk* have missed them all

after dinner drive

at dusk, shadows of night drape the world
hidden from sight are newborn fawns
wobbly legs, camouflaged body
they follow their doe onto dark asphalt

curves in the roadway hug tree lines
moonlight smothered by dark grey clouds
headlights embrace thirty feet dead ahead
until the front fender folds inward on impact

a mother shudders, then stops for a second,
collapses onto knees as her baby stands still
and my front lights go black from the shock
while i try to figure out what to do now

911 brings state police and the local tow —
a pistol shot ends a deer's misery and pain
while a fawn hobbles back into the woods
and shortly, a certain death from starvation

a calm drive home   scarred by an innocent death
the realization i killed a family is unsettling
all animals deserve to live their life to the fullest
a wasted life is a wasted life, two legs or four

old age meds

tiny small print on tiny small bottles
illegible to aged and tired eyes
magnifiers shake in wobbly hands
impossible to read, how many to take

the muscular hands of youth long gone
years of hard toil took their toll
fingers once dexterous, now are bent
arthritis inflames, and inflicts severe pain

pill bottles for seniors are hard to open
childproof containers stifle some folks
suffering for relief, you see them encased
miles from release, yet only inches away

blue origin

i watched it take off today
an all-female crew on board
experienced weightlessness
arrived in outer space

since the beginning of humanity
we secretly desired to fly in the air
aero-planes did it for a long time
now to float in the air is another thing

i grew up with a friend years ago
he also wanted to fly like a bird
a troubled childhood disrupted him
he jumped off a building to try to fly

silence

stones are mute
don't move, they
stiffly stand still

what's said, and
heard, without ears
offers relief to tears

when hearts bare all
that's
what tombstones do

shades of love

skin is like a box of crayons
all different colors and shades
some lighter, some darker
yet all do the same thing

none of them are good or bad colors
they're all the same when touched
as fingers wrap around a selected one
skin and crayons are similar in life

it's just skin, it's colored wax
nothing more, nothing less
doesn't matter who you love
you'll always win, it's just skin

family, friends, and bullies

my dinner plate is clean, empty of food
no one left to cook for me anymore —
they are all dead
they are all gone, to
somewhere   invisible
they have all vanished
parent's clothes and things, too
they left me alone
i have no childhood home
it has been demolished
my old neighborhood changed
they don't live here anymore
parents, friends, and bullies
flew away like pollen in the air
my irritants gone, dead
parents live forever in my memory
finally, i have peace in my head

sport fishing

fishing at the new jersey shore
is a gentleman's sport
no need for expensive rods and reels
or learning to tie a hook securely

a person can get almost any species
such as tuna, flounder, sea bass,
chilean bass, red snapper
shrimp, lobster, octopus, and so on

local restaurants try to serve fresh-caught
and you have a range of ambiance
from small fish market/restaurant shacks
with fishing trollers docked alongside

to fancy schmancy two-story ones
built on the beach
for diners viewing consumption
as they enjoy the ocean's bounty

if you want delicious fresh fish
the jersey shore is the place to dish

shadows

when birds sing
and flowers bloom
my shadow follows me
everywhere i go

on sunny days
i can never leave it behind
though sometimes
it foreshadows my every step

i lose it at night
when i go to bed
surprisingly
i never squish it

and i know
bigoted klansmen are upset
at the blackness of theirs
though i cherish mine

and i miss it
when rain pours down
on my lovely shadow,
to wash it away till tomorrow

new york city gentleman's club

her stage name is *butter*
when dancing
she melts
flows smoothly across
a hardwood stage
her kisses taste so sweet
a tongue you can almost eat

she lap dances for cash
oozes down with a crash
on a gentleman's hard lap
when finished took all his sap
fully emptied his tank
and took his cash to the bank

canned fish

he was young, late-teens,
while shopping, met an older woman
who started speaking softly —
intrigued instantly, smitten,
although he knew better,
went home with her, why not —
she seduced him, stayed hours,
then her girlfriend came home
and he soon found himself with her, too —
caught in bed between them
he felt like a sardine in a can
tightly packed together
two squishy fish on either side
oiled up, slipping all over the bed,
finally realized he was in over his head,
an experience he did not anticipate
it would be so extreme and exhausting,
but one he would never forget, and
years later, brought a smile to an old man
upon his deathbed

Thank you for reading my poetry.

For more of my books
please check out my website

www.CreativeFiction.net

on **Instagram** lookup
elliot_m_rubin
people poems

www.ingramcontent.com/pod-product-compliance
Lightning Source LLC
Chambersburg PA
CBHW071327130626
46556CB00004B/1786